10 Christmas Duets

For Beginning and Middle Level Instrumentalists

Arranged in concert key with five interchangeable parts

C Instruments in Bass Clef
C Instruments in Treble Clef
Bb Instruments in Treble Clef
Eb Instruments in Treble Clef
F Instruments in Treble Clef

arranged by Paul G. Young, Ph.D.

Createspace, An Amazon.com Company
Columbia, South Carolina
Available from Amazon.com and other retail outlets

ISBN-13: 978-1727751741
ISBN-10: 1727751744

Printed in the United States of America

Contents

Each selection includes a duet part for each of the following instrument groupings:

> C Instruments in Bass Clef (trombone, baritone, tuba, etc.)
> C Instruments in Treble Clef (flute, oboe, keyboard, etc.)
> Bb Instruments in Treble Clef (Bb clarinet and trumpet, tenor sax)
> Eb Instruments in Treble Clef (alto sax, baritone sax, alto clarinet, etc.)
> F Instruments in Treble Clef (F horn)

The duet parts are transposed in concert key. One C Flute could play with one Bb Clarinet, or small numbers of players could be assigned to duet Part I or Part II.

These duets would work well with beginning and middle level bands, especially those groups with imbalanced or missing instrumentation. Many of the duets could be prepared by students independently on their own for showcasing during programs. They also work well for student(s) and private teacher for studies in a studio setting.

About the Duets

Away in a Manger – first published in the late nineteenth century and popular throughout the English-speaking world. It is one of most popular carols in Britain. The tune has long been associated with German religious reformer Martin Luther, the carol is now thought to be wholly American in origin. Another tune using the same name was composed by James Ramsey Murray in 1887.

Deck the Halls – a Welsh carol found in a musical manuscript by harpist John Parry dating back to the 1700s. Originally, carols were dances and not songs.

God Rest Ye Merry Gentlemen – one of the oldest surviving English carols. It dates to the 16th century or earlier. The tune is in the minor mode. The carol is referred to in Charles Dickens' *A Christmas Carol.*

Jingle Bells – one of the best-known and commonly sung American songs. It was first published by James Lord Pierpont (1822–1893) in 1857. The song was originally intended for the Thanksgiving season. A plaque at 19 High Street in the center of Medford Square in Medford, Massachusetts, commemorates the "birthplace" of *Jingle Bells.*

Jolly Old Saint Nicholas – originated with a poem by Emily Huntington Miller (1833-1913) and published as "Lilly's Secret" in The Little Corporal Magazine in December 1865. The song's lyrics have also been attributed to Benjamin Hanby who wrote a similar song in the 1860s, *Up on the Housetop*. The music has been attributed to John Piersol McCaskey, a school principal and former Mayor of Lancaster, Pennsylvania, who claimed to have written the song in 1867.

O Christmas Tree (O Tannenbaum) – the tune is a 16th century German folk tune. It became associated with the traditional Christmas tree by the early 20th century and is sung today as a Christmas carol.

Silent Night – first performed on Christmas Eve 1818 at St. Nicholas Parish Church in the village of Oberndorf which is in present-day Austria. Father Joseph Mohr wrote the lyrics "Stille Nacht" in 1816. The melody was composed by Franz Gruber, a schoolmaster and organist, when Mohr brought the words to Gruber and asked him to compose a melody and guitar accompaniment for the Christmas Eve mass. *Silent Night* was declared an intangible cultural heritage by UNESCO in 2011.

Still, Still, Still – an anonymous Austrian folk tune which appeared for the first time in 1865 in a folksong collection of Maria Vinzenz Süß (1802–1868), founder of the Salzburg Museum. The words describe the peace of the infant Jesus and his mother as the baby is sung to sleep.

Up on the Housetop – written by Benjamin Hanby in 1864. As a secular Christmas song, it is preceded only by *Jingle Bells* (1857). It is also considered the first Yuletide song to focus primarily on Santa Claus. Hanby was born in 1833 near Rushville, Ohio. He was the son of a minister involved with the Underground Railroad.

We Wish You a Merry Christmas – a popular English Christmas carol whose early history is unclear. It is missing from The Oxford Book of Carols (1928). Its origin is from an English tradition in which wealthy people gave Christmas treats to the carolers on Christmas Eve.

Away in a Manger

Duet for C Instruments in Bass Clef

William J. Kirkpatrick (1895)

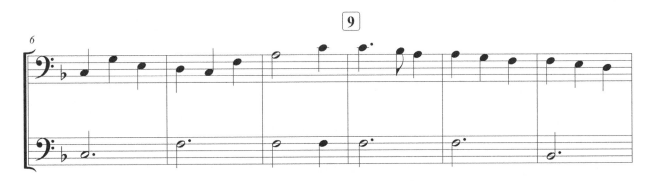

Away in a Manger

Duet for C Instruments in Treble Clef

William J. Kirkpatrick (1895)

Away in a Manger

Duet for Bb Instruments in Treble Clef

William J. Kirkpatrick (1895)

Away in a Manger

Duet for Eb Instruments in Treble Clef

William J. Kirkpatrick (1895)

Away in a Manger

Duet for F Instruments in Treble Clef

William J. Kirkpatrick (1895)

Deck the Halls

Duet for C Instruments in Bass Clef

Welsh Carol

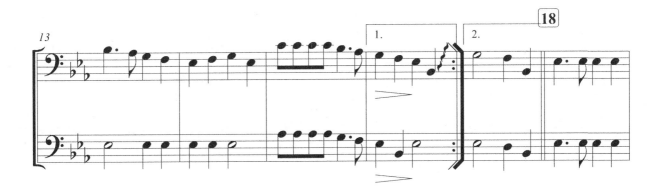

Deck the Halls

Duet for C Instruments in Treble Clef

Welsh Carol

Deck the Halls

Duet for Bb Instruments in Treble Clef

Welsh Carol

Deck the Halls

Duet for Eb Instruments in Treble Clef

Welsh Carol

Deck the Halls

Duets for F Instruments in Treble Clef

♩ = 120

Welsh Carol

God Rest You Merry Gentlemen

Duet for C Instruments in Bass Clef

16th Century English Carol

God Rest Ye Merry Gentlemen

Duet for C Instruments in Treble Clef

16th Century English Carol

God Rest Ye Merry Gentlemen

Duet for Bb Instruments in Treble Clef

16th Century English Carol

God Rest Ye Merry Gentlemen

Duet for Eb Instruments in Treble Clef

16th Century English Carol

God Rest Ye Merry Gentlemen

Duet for F Instruments in Treble Clef

16th Century English Carol

-17-

Jingle Bells

Duet for C Instruments in Bass Clef

James Lord Pierpont (1857)

Jingle Bells

Duet for C Instruments in Treble Clef

James Lord Pierpont (1857)

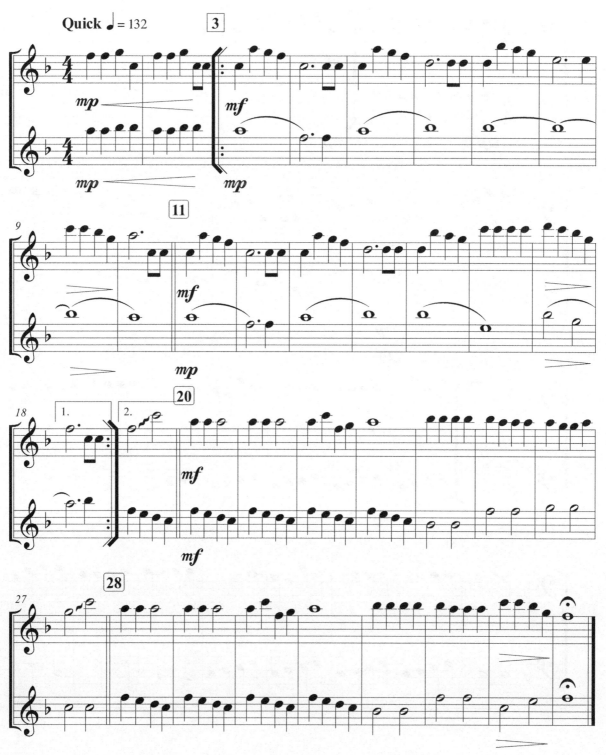

Jingle Bells

Duet for Bb Instruments in Treble Clef

James Lord Pierpont (1857)

Jingle Bells

Duet for Eb Instruments in Treble Clef

James Lord Pierpoint (1857)

Jingle Bells

Duet for F Instruments in Treble Clef

James Lord Pierpont (1857)

Jolly Old Saint Nicholas

Duet for C Instruments in Bass Clef

Traditional Carol

Jolly Old Saint Nicholas

Duet for C Instruments in Treble Clef

Traditional Carol

Jolly Old Saint Nicholas

Duet for Bb Instruments in Treble Clef

Traditional Carol

Jolly Old Saint Nicholas

Duet for Eb Instruments in Treble Clef

Traditional Carol

Jolly Old Saint Nicholas

Duet for F Instruments in Treble Clef

Traditional Carol

O Christmas Tree (O Tannenbaum)

Duet for C Instruments in Bass Clef

German Carol

O Christmas Tree (O Tannenbaum)

Duet for C Instruments in Treble Clef

German Carol

O Christmas Tree (O Tannenbaum)

Duet for Bb Instruments in Treble Clef

German Carol

O Christmas Tree (O Tannenbaum)

Duet for Eb Instruments in Treble Clef

German Carol

O Christmas Tree (O Tannenbaum)

Duet for F Instruments in Treble Clef

German Carol

Silent Night

Duet for C Instruments in Bass Clef

Franz Gruber (1818)

Silent Night

Duet for C Instruments in Treble Clef

Franz Gruber (1818)

Silent Night

Duet for Bb Instruments in Treble Clef

Franz Gruber (1818)

Silent Night

Duet for Eb Instruments in Treble Clef

Franz Gruber (1818)

Silent Night

Duet in F Instruments in Treble Clef

Franz Gruber (1818)

Still, Still, Still

Duet for C Instruments in Bass Clef

19th Century Austrian Carol & Lullaby

Still, Still, Still

Duet for C Instruments in Treble Clef

19th Century Austrian Carol and Lullaby

Still, Still, Still

Duet for Bb Instruments in Treble Clef

19th Century Austrian Carol and Lullaby

Still, Still, Still

Duet for Eb Instruments in Treble Clef

19th Century Austrian Carol and Lullaby

Still, Still, Still

Duet for F Instruments in Treble Clef

19th Century Austrian Carol and Lullaby

Up on the Housetop

Duet for C Instruments in Bass Clef

B.R. Hanby (1864)

Allegro ♩ = 100

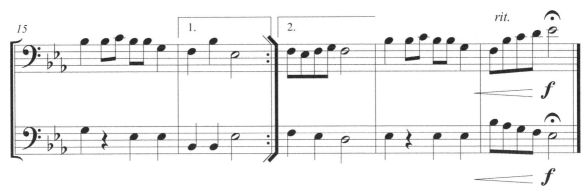

Up on the Housetop

Duet for C Instruments in Treble Clef

B. R. Hanby (1864)

Up in the Housetop

Duet for Bb Instruments in Treble Clef

B. R. Hanby (1864)

Allegro ♩ = 100

Up on the Housetop

Duet for Eb Instruments in Treble Clef

B. R. Hanby (1864)

Up on the Housetop

Duet for F Instruments in Treble Clef

B. R. Hanby (1864)

We Wish You a Merry Christmas

Duet for C Instruments in Bass Clef

English Carol

We Wish You a Merry Christmas

Duet for C Instruments in Treble Clef

English Carol

We Wish You a Merry Christmas

Duet for Bb Instruments in Treble Clef

English Carol

We Wish You a Merry Christmas

Duet for Eb Instruments in Treble Clef

English Carol

We Wish You a Merry Christmas

Duet for F Instruments in Treble Clef

English Carol

About the Arranger

Dr. Paul G. Young, Ph.D., has worked as a high school band director, elementary and junior high classroom teacher (grades 4, 5, and 7), nearly 20 years as an elementary school principal, and as an executive director of an afterschool program, all near the area of Lancaster, Ohio. For more than 45 years he has also served as an adjunct professor of music classes at Ohio University-Lancaster campus. He holds bachelor and masters degrees in music from the Ohio University School of Music. His doctorate, in Educational Administration, is also from Ohio University, Athens, Ohio.

He served in leadership roles with both the National Association of Elementary School Principals (NAESP) and the National AfterSchool Association (NAA). He was elected as president of the 30,000 member NAESP in 2002-2003. He served as a member of the NAA Board of Directors starting in 2008 before becoming NAA's President and CEO in 2010. He retired from association work in 2012. He has written extensively on the topic of school and afterschool alignment, led training workshops throughout the country, and played an influential role in the development of practical, evidence-based alignment strategies for school leaders and afterschool professionals. He is the author of *Enhancing the Professional Practice of Music Teachers: 101 Tips that Principals Want Music Teachers to Know and Do* (Rowman and Littlefield-Education) as well as several other books for principals, music teachers, and afterschool professionals.

Dr. Young and his wife, Gertrude, a retired music teacher, live in Lancaster, Ohio. They have two adult daughters and sons-in-law. Katie and her husband, Jon Steele, live in Glendale, Wisconsin, where she is the principal oboist with the Milwaukee Symphony. She previously performed with the New World Symphony and the Florida Orchestra. Jon is the Field Marketing Director for the Eastern U.S. for Medshape, an Atlanta-based medical group. Mary Ellen and her husband, Eric, live in Glen Ellyn, Illinois. Mary Ellen is Senior Market Development Manager for McGraw Hill-Higher Education and Eric is a designer for Looney and Associates, Chicago.

Dr. and Mrs. Young enjoy their four grandchildren - Nora Rahn, Charles Steele, Evan Rahn, and Jonathan Paul "Jack" Steele and hope they each grow to enjoy a life filled with musical experiences.

Made in the USA
Monee, IL
25 August 2023

41625789R00037